CAREER IN
HOME ECONOMICS
IN THE FOOD INDUSTRY

FAMILY AND CONSUMER SCIENCES PROFESSIONALS

FOOD IS THE MOST BASIC OF HUMAN NEEDS so it is no wonder that the food industry is the largest industry in the world. Food production and distribution in the US are dominated by multinational corporations like Kraft, Nestle, Sysco, and General Mills, as well as restaurant chains that circle the globe. The industry employs millions of people, including home economists. These are highly trained professionals who are able to combine their passion for food, knack for science, and creative flair to create food that is delicious, healthy, safe, affordable, and interesting.

This is a very diverse field that offers numerous career paths. Home economists conduct research and experiments in labs, cook up new recipes, design and test new kitchen equipment, determine what food policies best address public health and safety, demonstrate cooking techniques, and write about their favorite subject – food. With culinary skills and proper training, these professionals can become test kitchen cooks, research chefs, recipe developers, newspaper columnists, TV cooking show producers, food stylists, or food technologists. Because the food industry is massive, there is also an opportunity to specialize in certain foods or beverages, or specific kinds of employers.

There is plenty of opportunity, particularly for those who are innovative and think outside the box. Major food companies, large media outlets, consulting firms, advertising agencies, universities, large restaurant chains, and government agencies are always looking for imaginative home economists. They all offer good salaries and job stability, as well as a chance to achieve great personal and professional satisfaction. Many home economists choose to freelance, obtaining projects through their network of contacts in the industry. For them, the pay is even greater than a salary would be, and the freedom to work when and how they choose more than compensates for the lack of stability.

Becoming a home economist requires a college education in most cases. A bachelor's degree in home economics (now commonly known as Family and Consumer Sciences or FCS) is all it takes to qualify for most positions. Some areas of advanced research or teaching at the university level demand graduate degrees. Hands-on experience gives new graduates an advantage when looking for their first jobs, but that experience is easy to get through internships, volunteering, or working part time in any situation that involves food.

If you love food, have some basic cooking skills, and want to work in a more relaxed environment than the chaotic atmosphere of a restaurant kitchen, home economics could be the answer. It is a fun, exciting career that can provide a lifetime of pleasure and fulfillment.

WHAT YOU CAN DO NOW

MAKE THE MOST OF HIGH SCHOOL. Naturally, you will want to take advantage of any classes that may be offered in Family and Consumer Sciences. Beyond the obvious, there are several subject areas that will be beneficial to your career. Communications skills are important in every area of FCS. English, speech, journalism, and even drama classes are all good choices. Those interested in food technology should focus on science courses, particularly chemistry, biology, and physics. Start collecting college catalogs as early as possible to make sure you will have all the required courses for admission.

Shop for a college

Not all FCS programs are alike. You will want to choose one that matches your future career goals. Most FCS graduates obtain their first jobs through the college career center. Talk with the placement counselor at any schools that interest you. Make sure the school has a good reputation for placing graduates in the kind of job you want.

Learn to cook

It is not a skill you can master by reading about it. You will eventually learn about the chemistry of food, but start with the basics. Specialty food stores, community centers, adult education programs, and some restaurants offer cooking classes. You can also learn by following along with the many cooking shows on cable TV. Practice your skills any chance you get.

Get competitive

There are many recipes and cooking contests open to amateurs. Stretch yourself and look for those that stress originality. Simply entering and competing in contests will look good on your college application. Winning contests will get the attention of any food products company that is hiring.

Get familiar with food

Look for a summer job or part-time work in a restaurant, nursing home, or hospital commissary. Make sure the job is in the kitchen actually handling food. If you cannot find a paying job, there are always volunteer positions available.

Develop your personal style

Read food blogs, cookbooks, and food magazines to stay current with food trends. You will also find industry news on professional association websites.

HISTORY OF THE PROFESSION

THE FIELD OF HOME ECONOMICS emerged in the late 19th century. It was a movement led by Ellen Swallow Richards, who made a big splash at the 1893 World's Fair in Chicago. There she designed the Rumford Kitchen, a tiny space of her own where she served healthy meals to fair goers and provided nutrition education to anyone who would listen. Richards had been invited to participate in the demonstration kitchen in the Women's Building. She refused the offer, stating that nutrition information should be for everyone, not just women. The information she provided was based on her own chemistry research conducted at the Massachusetts Institute of Technology (MIT). She was the first woman to attend MIT and its first instructor in this subject.

During the 10 years following Richard's public debut in Chicago, she met regularly with a group of educators of like mind to explore the new discipline that came to be known as "home economics." The group's goal was to elevate the new field into a legitimate profession. One way to do that was to form an education and scientific association that would define and set standards for the profession. They did so in 1909 with the founding of the American Home Economics Association (AHEA). The association, which is now known as the American Association of Family and Consumer Sciences, is still today the leading professional organization in the field.

Early in the 20th century, the AHEA was successful in getting two pieces of key legislation passed that would allow home economists to conduct research and teach in institutions of higher education. The Smith-Lever Act of 1914 and the Smith-Hughes Act of 1917 provided funding to expand instructional work in rural communities, and to develop and teach a home economics curriculum on the campuses of most state colleges.

Early home economics classes were intended to prepare young women for their duties in the home. Instruction focused on nutrition and the creation of healthy environments. Classes were first offered in the United States, but soon appeared in Canada, Europe, and the rest of the world.

Food was always a major concern of home economics. One of the movement's primary goals was to apply modern principles of science and efficiency to food production. When the field first began, the quality of the food supply was unreliable. Basic ingredients were inconsistent and the lack of refrigeration made it impossible to ensure even basic standards of sanitation. Kitchen equipment was primitive and cookbooks were not in wide use. Most people prepared food-using methods passed down through the family. It was not until after World War I that indoor plumbing, electricity, and gas stoves became widely available. In the modern world, those basic things are taken for granted, but 100 years ago they were marvelous advances that made it possible to have safe and healthy food in most homes.

Although training in home economics was originally meant to prepare women for homemaking, it was not long before professionals in the field sought to use their specific knowledge outside the domestic sphere. Home economists were having an important impact on food and nutrition practices in the US, and college faculty members were making major research contributions to the field of food science. In 1924, the AHEA formed a new section known as Home Economists in Business (HEIB). Most of the HEIB members started out working for food companies like Washburn Crosby (later General Mills) and Kellogg's, or for trade associations such as the Institute of American Meat Packers and the National Dairy Council. Many wrote on nutrition and food preparation for newspapers and women's magazines, or helped manufacturers design modern, more reliable kitchen equipment.

Throughout the 20th century, the field expanded into a broad spectrum of careers within the food industry. As various professional roles were legitimized, home economists found employment in iconic institutions, such as the Girl Scouts of America, Campbell's Soup Company, and Macy's. They distributed scientific information to the public through radio shows, such as "Listen to Nutrition."

As more and more women faced the reality of needing to earn a living, colleges responded by educating students about career options after graduation. School counseling centers started to match graduates with the growing number of companies eager to hire graduates with home economics training. The counseling centers also provided access to alumnae networks that could help secure employment. By the end of World War II, home economists had become recognized and sought after for their expertise in a variety of food-related fields.

By the end of the 20th century, food had become a national obsession. Celebrity chefs inspired amateur cooks through TV shows, books, magazines, and websites. Food writers had to share the media space with a growing number of food bloggers – some of whom had millions of followers on YouTube. It became customary for anyone with a smartphone to document and share their experiences with food via social media. Today, our national love affair with food has created a myriad of opportunities for highly trained, independent experts in all areas of food production, marketing, and distribution.

WHERE YOU WILL WORK

HOME ECONOMISTS WORK IN A VERY LARGE VARITY of work settings. Roughly half are in the food manufacturing industry, while 13 percent work in research and development and 8 percent work for the federal government. The types of employers who hire home economists include:

- Food and beverage manufacturers and distributors

- Large retailers

- Marketing firms and advertising agencies

- Community and government agencies

- Restaurant chains

- Hospitals and assisted-care facilities

- Private research laboratories contracted by food manufacturers

The biggest employers of home economists are companies with household names, such as General Mills and Coca-Cola. Big food manufacturers like this may have a large number of home economists on the payroll working in various departments throughout the organization. Most of them operate test kitchens staffed with dozens of home economists tasked with developing and testing new products and recipes.

Other large employers are in the business of manufacturing home cooking and commercial food processing equipment. Companies like Cuisinart and DeLonghi are well known for producing quality, innovative kitchenware for consumers. Other companies, like Hughes and Horizon Bradco, are not so well known because they only manufacture equipment for commercial use.

Traditionally, home economists were in the business of educating the public. This tradition continues in the form of public relations. Employers in this arena include the public relations departments of large companies and independent public relations firms that serve the food industry trade associations, such as the National Dairy Council, North American Meat Processors, and the Specialty Food Association.

Home economists can also be found in academia. Those who are university faculty members often conduct research in addition to their teaching duties. Very often, government agencies turn to universities to help with special research projects. For example, the food pyramid was developed at Tufts University for the US Department of Agriculture (USDA).

Depending on their role, home economists can be found anywhere from a factory floor to a TV studio. Most work in an office, laboratory, or kitchen. With the exception of factories and processing plants, which can be noisy and uncomfortable, the work environment for most home economists is modern, clean, and bright.

Home economists can work on a part-time, full-time, or contractual basis. There are some who are freelancers, able to set their own schedules and work as little or as much as they like. Freelancers are in the minority, though. Most are salaried employees with the usual standard work schedule. Some positions require evening work and others involve travel. The amount of travel may vary, but there is often the opportunity to travel around the country and even internationally, visiting food sources, meeting with clients, giving presentations, and participating in trade shows. Some positions require extensive travel that may mean spending half of your time on the road.

THE WORK YOU WILL DO

HOME ECONOMICS OFFERS A RANGE of career options in the food industry. To some degree, all job roles involve the creation or improvement of food and kitchen products that are tasty and healthy, or useful and marketable. Most professionals in this career field are involved in research and development for either the individual consumer and for institutional use. In some cases, it is simply a matter of coming up with fresh new variations of existing menu items. It may mean inventing entirely new food products or kitchen equipment. The home economist views things as the consumer would, determining what tastes better, what works best in the kitchen, and what is needed that is not currently available.

Depending on the employer or area of interest, home economists might do the following:

- Develop new food products
- Create and taste test new recipes
- Write about food
- Design and test new kitchen equipment
- Discuss food issues with consumers
- Study consumer behavior and promote products
- Conduct research
- Teach at high schools, colleges and universities
- Provide food to groups of people in schools, hotels, hospitals, and other industrial or commercial institutions

Among the many kinds of jobs for home economists in the food industry, most fall into one of these specialized areas.

Food Technology

Food technologists usually work for companies that produce food. They are involved early in the process, often conducting experiments and producing sample products. The goal is to develop foods that are safer and healthier for consumption. They also design the processes and machinery for mass-producing products with a consistent flavor and texture.

Food technologists also analyze the nutritional content of foods and manage product recalls. While researching new food sources, they look for substitutes for harmful and unhealthy ingredients and ways to improve food quality. Sometimes they conduct consumer surveys to determine satisfaction with certain food products or to discover emerging trends.

Food technologists are responsible for the safety and hygiene of food production. They must ensure that food products meet government and industry standards for quality, and that manufacturing areas comply with government regulations regarding sanitation and waste management.

Recipe Development and Testing

Recipe developers are the artists working behind the scenes to create your favorite foods. Their job is to come up with the exact ingredients and in the right quantities to produce dishes on restaurant menus or in your own kitchen. Some of these specialists work for food companies, creating recipes that would entice a consumer to buy more of a certain food product. For example, recipe developers at Campbell's come up with 1,500 recipes each year for the purpose of selling more cans of soup.

Some recipe developers create recipes for individuals with specific health or dietary concerns. Others come up with recipes for magazine and cookbook publishers. In many cases, they must also cook the dish for photo shoots. This often requires multiple attempts since the food in the photo must be perfect and appealing enough to sell the product.

Test Kitchen Staff

Large food companies and food magazines operate test kitchens to develop new kinds of food, create new recipes, or try out new food processing equipment. The most common goal is to perfect a recipe so that it can be easily replicated by anyone. This is more complicated than it sounds. Testing recipes is a science, where the weighing, measuring, and timing of everything must be precise. It is not unusual for testers to cook the same recipe 100 times before getting it right.

Test kitchens are staffed by teams, each tasked with specific responsibilities. The kitchen manager directs the test cooks, assistant cooks, and taste testers. The test cooks shop for ingredients, conduct any necessary research, gather needed tools and equipment, and prepare the dish. Under the supervision of the test cook, assistants and tasters do the prep work, organize groceries, clean and calibrate equipment, and help out during photo shoots.

Food Product Development

Food product developers, commonly known as research chefs or R&D chefs, create new foods for restaurant chains and food manufacturers. They often work in corporate kitchens, developing recipes for the packaged food products found in grocery stores. They apply knowledge of chemistry to their craft to create items that balance taste, texture, perishability and marketability. They often collaborate with food scientists to find better ways to retain the flavor, freshness, consistency, and nutritional content of mass-produced food products. They are also experts in food preservation. They may study the shelf life of packaged foods or help devise packaging materials that prevent the growth of the microorganisms that cause foodborne illness.

Food Media

Food media jobs include writers, stylists, and photographers. For a lucky few, it also includes TV personalities like celebrity chef Bobby Flay. Many media specialists are freelancers, taking on projects from various publishers and television producers, or producing their own YouTube channels and blogs. Others are salaried staff for major newspapers or magazines such as Bon Appetit or Food & Wine, or for food content TV channels. Food styling and photography are in high demand for online food content sites as well as consumer sites like Instagram and Pinterest.

Food media job descriptions vary widely. Writers may be critics, cookbook authors, ghostwriters for celebrities, or scriptwriters for television or online food content channels. Stylists work for photographers, creating mouth-watering dishes that look like masterpieces. Photographs of food end up in magazines, newspapers, books, TV shows, and advertisements. It is extremely creative work that involves preparing the food, then staging it to make it appear most appealing. Food stylists are hired to do the shopping and prep work for celebrity chefs.

Not all home economists in the food industry spend their time in the kitchen. Some work in public relations, promoting products, delivering speeches, and setting up exhibits at trade shows. Others are involved in food safety, consumer services, food policy, and nonprofit services. Government agencies rely on home economists to help protect the public's health by laboratory testing of food products for dangerous pathogens. Home economists at large food companies create public awareness of company products and foster good will through contact with consumers who call the toll-free numbers typically found on product packages.

Food policy work is carried out at trade associations. Food policies are generally designed to keep food safe, healthy, and affordable. Nonprofit workers typically provide educational services, and help to produce and provide access to better food for those in need. For example, a home economist might plan meals for organizations like Meals on Wheels.

HOME ECONOMISTS TELL THEIR OWN STORIES

I Am a Recipe Developer

"My job is the ultimate creative experience. I consider myself an artist because I start with an original idea and develop it from scratch. The recipes I dream up may be for a cookbook, restaurant menu, or a special event. Occasionally, they become mass produced consumer products available in your local grocery store.

Like everyone else in this business, I started by learning to cook. At some point, I was hooked. I began to obsessively buy books, magazines, ingredients, and utensils. At least once or twice a week, I would try new restaurants, then go home to deconstruct what I'd eaten.

My first job was recipe testing. I thought it was the greatest job in the world, being paid to cook, but I wasn't being paid to enjoy the sheer pleasure of cooking. I was essentially a problem solver, and I had to identify the problems first before figuring out the solutions. The goal was always the same: make sure that anyone – a reader cooking at home, manufacturer, restaurant chef, or friend – could reproduce the dish with the same perfect results. There was no spontaneous creativity involved, rather serious attention to detail. All that testing later became a vital part of my success as a recipe developer. My appreciation for the details is what makes my recipes successful.

I spent nearly 10 years working as a recipe developer for a food magazine. It was an intensely creative environment. The magazine was bought out and eventually morphed into something completely different. At that point, I became a freelancer. Now I depend on my network of colleagues to send projects my way. As an independent, I have created recipes for a TV chef, written articles for food magazines, developed recipes for cookbooks, and helped upscale restaurants 'refresh' their menus.

My advice to anyone who is thinking about getting into this kind of work is to have confidence in yourself. I have had my share of failures and have lived through the occasional disaster. You will, too. It is part of the learning process. Trust your own experiences rather than cookbooks. Always be questioning how the recipe came together and what you could do to make it better. Figure out what techniques click for you and develop your own style. After all the frustration and hard work, there will be a market for your expertise."

I Am a Freelance R&D Chef

"To be a home economist means different things to different people in the food industry. I generally consider myself a link between the consumer and industry. Because I freelance, I wear many different hats in my work. I spend my time bouncing between R&D, production, marketing, and sales. My work is usually a combination of developing prototypes, production meetings, test runs, market research, and preparing documentation related to organic, gluten-free, and other specialty labels.

There is no typical day. I could be on a plane flying to a client presentation one day and setting up photo shoots the next. If I am working for a kitchen appliance manufacturer, I research cost, efficiency, materials availability, and sustainability of the product. When I am employed by a marketing department, job tasks might include writing, blogging, social networking, cooking demonstrations, recipe development, food styling, or product evaluation. Basically, I am responsible for making the company's product a star.

Home economics does not have to mean being restricted to a kitchen. It can take you to some exotic locations. I have seen the world and regardless of cultural differences, I have discovered that issues like consumerism, nutrition, food security, and efficient use of limited resources are a global concern. The work is not just about creating delicious recipes either. It's about ensuring that a client's food product or kitchen equipment is the best it can be and feeling good about encouraging consumers to buy them."

I Am a Test Kitchen Intern

"I never expected to have a career that allowed me to explore the creative side of cooking. I was in the military until an injury forced me to leave active duty. With nothing much to do while recovering, I started cooking. I was soon hooked and started reading every food publication I could get my hands on. The Food Network was always on and I'd fantasize about being Anthony Bourdain. I never thought that I could love something so much and actually turn it into a job. On a whim one day, I called up a local college and started my career education two months later.

Through my school, I was able to pursue an internship at the city newspaper. I was surprised to learn that they had a test kitchen with around 20 interns from various schools around the country rotating through at any given time. Collectively, we test every recipe that's published in the paper. The fun part is creating new recipes and shooting step-by-step demonstrations for videos on the paper's website. It's all fun and games until I realized that there are tens of thousands of readers counting on accurate information that will make their next family gathering perfect.

As an intern, I receive priceless hands-on training in the finer points of recipe testing and development. I have also learned food styling techniques and get to interact with chefs, writers, and food professionals of all kinds. My days are filled with phone calls to chefs, grocery store runs, and cooking. Lots and lots of cooking. We work in teams of two to deconstruct and recreate recipes, often testing dozens of times to get a recipe right. We check everything from start to finish, then proofread it and send it on its way. To see a recipe finally published is the most rewarding part of working here."

PERSONAL QUALIFICATIONS

MOST PEOPLE ARE ATTRACTED TO THIS career because they are passionate about food. That is a good start. A genuine interest in food will keep the work interesting day after day. But there is much more to this career than being a foodie. The most successful professionals in this field are able to combine their passion for food with a knack for science and a flair for creativity. There are also a few certain traits that they all have in common.

Communications Skills

Excellent communication and presentation skills are critical for every type of work in this field. Writing is a primary activity in most positions. Depending on your role, you may be required to write reports, instructions, news releases, labels, user guides, or sales training manuals. If you are involved in food technology or research, you will need to explain your studies in a way that makes sense to your employer or clients. Strong verbal skills are a must. You may be interacting with different departments such as research, sales, production, marketing, or advertising. Giving presentations is another common job requirement. You may be called upon to address consumer groups, make product demonstrations, give instructions to testers, demonstrate cooking techniques, or describe product features to sales staff.

People Skills

While it is necessary to have the self-discipline to work independently, most people in this field interact regularly with other people. It is common to work as part of a team where cooperation is essential. Often, the work involves multiple teams or departments. At the very least, you will need the support of people from other departments. You will need to hone your listening skills and be open to different ideas. Building effective working relationships will open doors as you advance in your career.

Initiative

This work is all about new things – new products, new recipes, new methods. Success depends on taking the lead and trying out new ideas without fear of being wrong. Failure is an inevitable part of the process. It often takes great patience and determination to get through a project.

Critical Thinking

People in this field are natural problem-solvers. Their powers of observation and attention to details are needed for every project, whether it is perfecting a recipe or testing a product for shelf life.

ATTRACTIVE FEATURES

THERE ARE MANY SATISFYING ASPECTS of working as a home economist in the food industry. It is a great choice for anyone with a creative flair who loves food. The work is fun, and it is especially exciting when new recipes or products succeed. Imagine dreaming up a new menu item that goes national. Millions of people across the country will be enjoying food created by you!

Professionals in this field are paid well for working with food. Some freelancers earn over $100 an hour, and those who negotiate a percentage of the profits can make a fortune when a new product is a hit. The benefits of this work extend beyond earnings. The opportunity to be innovative is always available.

When your original recipe or product succeeds, there is the enjoyment of seeing people eating and enjoying your creations.

Working in a test kitchen or as a research chef is nothing like cooking in a restaurant. Restaurant workers have to work evenings and weekends, and the fast pace can create terrible stress. Most home economists in the food industry work regular eight-hour days. Even when there is a deadline to meet, they can work at a relaxed pace. They also work without close supervision, unlike their restaurant counterparts who are directed by executive chefs with demanding expectations.

For those with big dreams, there is always the chance of finding fame and fortune in this field. Research chefs and those involved in media can receive national or international acclaim when they create a popular new food product or host their own TV series.

The food industry also offers diversity. The variety of foods and drinks is endless. There is something that appeals to every taste and desire, including your own. You can choose your favorite kind of food and specialize, developing completely new products and improving on some old favorites. In fact, having specialized expertise is a big plus when searching for the best jobs.

UNATTRACTIVE ASPECTS

HOME ECONOMISTS IN THE FOOD INDUSTRY are generally happy about their career choice. There are, however, a few negative aspects to consider. First and foremost is the work schedule. Some jobs enjoy a regular schedule, with maybe an occasional deadline that requires putting in extra hours. There are also some jobs that routinely require irregular hours. Food stylists, for example, often have to stand for more than 12 hours at a time to complete a photo shoot. Then there may not be another shoot for several days. Consultants also experience erratic schedules that can easily run long into the evening or on weekends. This is usually due to extremely detailed and demanding client specifications.

Self-employment is common in this field. It offers great potential for earning more than an average salary, but it can take a while – sometimes years – to realize that potential. In the meantime, there may be periods of little or no income. Freelancers (self-employed people) often have to take day jobs unrelated to food in order to make a living until they make a name for themselves.

The opportunity to travel is attractive to many, but not everyone is willing to spend half their time away from home. Roles that require heavy travel can be hard on anyone with a family.

There is stiff competition for some jobs. If you dream of being the next celebrity chef, stand in line. Most beginners have to start out in low-level positions that are not exactly what they trained for. It takes time to build a career in this field, but determination and hard work will pay off in the long run.

The work can get tedious. You might have to test a recipe a hundred times to get it right, but there is great satisfaction in finally producing a dish that is perfectly delicious.

EDUCATION AND TRAINING

MOST HOME ECONOMISTS ARE college graduates who have completed a four year Bachelor of Science (BS or BSc) degree. Depending on the college, the program of study may be called Home Economics, Human Ecology, Family and Consumer Sciences, Nutrition and Food Sciences, or Consumer Studies. Programs typically include a combination of liberal arts education and home economics subjects. The liberal arts courses generally cover natural and social sciences, humanities, and the arts. The home economics courses focus on the specific knowledge needed to prepare for the profession. In addition to classroom instruction, internships are mandatory. This degree will satisfy most employers of food developers, recipe developers, and test kitchen staff.

There are educational alternatives for other positions. Recipe testers, both cooks and tasters, can get started with only a high school diploma. They do, however, need to demonstrate excellent reading and comprehension skills as well as basic cooking abilities.

Most employers of food and/or recipe developers require home economics degrees. Some will also hire graduates from culinary institutes. A good culinary arts degree program stresses the art and science of inventing original and exciting new recipes for a variety of occasions and markets. The best programs encourage creativity, intuition and experimentation.

The work of a research chef requires a unique combination of science education and culinary training. Obtaining the necessary mixture of skills starts with a bachelor's degree in science with coursework in chemistry, nutrition, and food science. Alternatively, a research chef can begin by pursuing culinary training from a school accredited by the American Culinary Federation. In this case, certification is highly advised.

A bachelor's degree is needed to become a food technologist. Those working in advanced research will need a master's or doctoral degree. Depending on the specific job role and employer, there are several choices of major, including food technology, chemistry, biology, engineering (food or mechanical), agriculture, or business. Bachelor degree programs cover the principles of management, science, and marketing, blended into one field of study that focuses on food values. Courses include food preservation, chemistry, nutrition, food processes, fermentation, flavor chemistry, sanitation, and marketing. Packaging is also covered, as it pertains to preserving food and improving food quality. Internship and research experiences are generally required for graduation.

Graduate programs usually combine classroom instruction, laboratory research, and fieldwork. Doctoral programs are heavy in research methodology courses, preparing students to research and hypothesize solutions to packaging and preservation problems. There are also food communication courses that teach you how to promote new products through media outlets, and food distribution courses that cover preservation during transportation and distribution to stores.

Food writers, journalists, stylists, and others in food media can choose between a home economics degree or a good liberal arts education. Either way, the emphasis should be on writing, English literature, and the arts. Magazine editors looking for staff writers prefer to see a journalism major. Most consider a combination of journalism and home economics ideal because it means the candidate could potentially be groomed for editorial positions.

Freelancers do not necessarily need a degree. A portfolio is the usual introductory tool. That does not mean education has no value. Aspiring freelancers should look for courses in food writing or food media.

Certification

The American Association of Family and Consumer Sciences (AAFCS) is the only national organization that offers certification for home economics professionals. This highly respected program promotes continuing education, professional growth, and excellence in the profession. The main benefit of certification is increased employment opportunities. To qualify, the applicant must have earned a bachelor's degree and pass an exam. Candidates are tested on general knowledge as well as mastery of the individual's chosen professional specialization.

Those focusing on food product development can become Certified Research Chefs. Certifying exams are conducted by the Research Chefs Association for those who meet education and experience requirements. Candidates must also demonstrate familiarity with food research and development.

EARNINGS

HOW MUCH HOME ECONOMISTS IN the food industry can expect to earn depends on several factors, the most important of which are area of specialty, type of employer, and geographic location.

Food Technologist

The median annual salary of food technologists is roughly $66,000. That is respectable income, but there is much upwardly mobile potential. After 10 years on the job, the typical salary only rises about 20 percent. That may be the reason so many food technologists move on to other positions after 20 years in this field. Food technologists can, however, improve their financial outlook by carefully choosing where to work. They can work in a wide variety of industries, and some pay considerably more than others. All require the same skills so moving into more profitable areas can be done without additional training. The highest salaries in the profession are offered by the federal government, where food technologists enjoy an average salary of $92,000 per year. Other higher-than-average yearly salaries include food product wholesalers ($77,000), seafood product preparation and packaging ($77,000), and scientific research and development services ($75,000).

Recipe Developer/Tester

Nationwide, recipe developers earn an average salary of $68,000. There is a big range though, starting at $40,000 for the lowest earners, and going as high as $120,000 on the top end. This is one job where the type of employer makes a huge difference in earnings. Recipe developers and testers are often hired by cookbook authors or publishers. In that situation, the pay is typically an hourly wage that amounts to little more than minimum wage. The story is not much better at magazines and newspapers – even large ones pay salaried employees between $15 and $20 an hour. Big food companies offer the best pay, where starting salaries for new employees is at least $40,000, with the promise of periodic raises and good benefits.

Test Kitchen Staff

Average earnings for people who work in test kitchens is hard to pin down because there are many freelancers, part-time employees, and interns. These are usually non-salaried workers who are paid hourly rates rather than annual salaries. Earnings range from minimum wage for interns to around $25 an hour for part-time, permanent employees. For full-time work, jobs start at $25,000 per year. That is for an assistant cook position that could develop into a higher- level job over time. At the top of the earnings chain are test kitchen managers. They typically earn more than $80,000 a year.

Food Writer (Food Media)

For food writers and food stylists, earnings depend on the type of media, whether they are salaried or freelance, and how popular the publication or show is. The average salary of a food stylist is $33,000 per year. Though there are a few companies that hire full-time in-house food stylists on salary, most of these professionals work as freelancers. Pay in the beginning can be spotty, but once established, a freelance food stylist can earn between $450 to $850 per day. That translates to an annual salary of over $200,000 if you get constant work.

The salary range for a food writer, ranges from $30,000 to $70,000. Technically, you do not need a degree to become a food writer, but it certainly helps. Those who have a degree in journalism or English as well as a home economics degree can secure a spot in the higher income range. Experience also goes a long way toward getting higher pay. A beginner probably will earn more than $20,000 the first year, while an experienced writer with 20 years in the industry can command as much as

$100,000 or more.

Food Product Developer/Research Chef

According to the Research Chefs Association, the salaries of research chefs can vary widely based on where they work, level of education, level of experience, and the specific responsibilities of the job. The average annual salary for these professionals is around $60,000. Experienced research chefs can earn as much as $30,000 more. Research chefs typically earn more than restaurant chefs due to the direct application of scientific knowledge in their work activities. The median salary of restaurant chefs is about $45,000.

Research chef is a specialty where professionals often prefer to work as consultants because they can usually get higher pay than their salaried colleagues. Some even negotiate for a cut from product sales. If the new product is a hit, the research chef who came up with the idea could enjoy a windfall.

Regional Differences

Salaries vary by geographic location. For example, food technologists working in Hawaii are paid an average salary of more than $100,000. That is the highest pay among all the states and districts. Other top-paying states include New Jersey, Massachusetts, Minnesota, and California. The average salary in those states ranges from $70,000 to $90,000. Compare that to similar positions in Oregon, Oklahoma, South Dakota, Nebraska, North Carolina, and Arkansas where the average salary hovers around the mid-$40,000s.

There are also specific metropolitan regions of the country that are particularly generous. The Santa Rosa, California area tops the list with an average annual salary of $135,000 for food technologists. Other top-earning regions include Bethesda, Columbus, Newark, and Cincinnati. Likewise, salaries for recipe developers vary widely by city. The average salary for this job in New York City, for example, is $105,000. That is more than 50 percent higher than the national average for the same type of work.

Salaried home economists usually receive benefit plans including the typical health and life insurance, retirement plans, and vacation and sick pay. Some employers provide reimbursement for continuing education. Profit sharing and bonuses are sometimes offered, amounting to as much as $10,000 annually. Freelancers are self-employed and therefore, are responsible for paying their own taxes and providing for their own retirement and health insurance.

OPPORTUNITIES

THE FIELD OF HOME ECONOMICS IS CHARACTERIZED by numerous career paths in the food industry. The best prospects are found in food technology, product development, marketing, test kitchens, and publishing. Most new jobs will stem from the need for new food products and the general increasing need for food science research.

Overall, employment levels for most job titles in this field are stable and job growth is on a par with other occupations. For example, job growth for food technologists is expected to be around 11 percent over the coming decade. It is about the same for research chefs.

Historically, most jobs for home economists working outside of the educational environment are found in major food companies like General Foods, Kellogg's Sysco, Nestle, Kraft, and Quaker. The food industry, which is now globalized, is the largest industry in the world. It generates roughly $5 trillion worldwide and accounts for 10 percent of the world's gross domestic product. With that kind of money at stake, it has become a highly competitive industry. Like all big corporations, those employing home economists continue to offer excellent compensation packages to attract the best candidates.

The corporate world is also where the best prospects for career advancement exist. Promotion within larger organizations typically leads to supervisory and management positions. For example, a typical career path for a food technologist might look like this:

- Development technologist
- Senior development technologist
- Project leader
- New product development manager

Bigger companies also offer more opportunities to move within the organization from one department to another. Those with expertise in particular areas have the edge. They can easily transition from one area to another where their specialist knowledge can be utilized.

Medium and smaller sized companies, however, have their advantages. They are good places for new graduates to start their careers because employees typically are given more responsibilities. It is the best way to obtain skills and experience across a range of areas quickly. However, to gain a promotion or get a salary increase, it may be necessary to move between employers. That may require relocation in some cases.

The best opportunities will be found in niche markets. There is a real need for home economists who have knowledge and expertise serving special groups of consumers. The hottest markets at the moment include special food needs of seniors, and those with health-related food needs, such as gluten-free diets for celiac patients or low-glycemic foods for diabetics.

The food industry is increasingly based on technology. People who take advantage of training opportunities to learn more about the technology of food will have a competitive edge for the best jobs.

GETTING STARTED

FINDING YOUR FIRST JOB IN THIS FIELD will take some planning and a little work. You will find positions advertised in your local newspaper or on employment websites, but there are numerous other ways to go about a job search. If you are smart, you will pursue more than one.

Get Some Experience

Nothing captures the attention of prospective employers more than experience. They like to know you have a realistic view of what the work is really about. Plus, having done actual hands-on work means that you have some skills to offer. There are three basic ways to get experience: internships, volunteering, and paid positions.

Most college programs provide opportunities to participate in internships. The competition can be tough though, so look for ways to create your opening. You can arrange for internships in the kitchen of a local restaurant or with a chef or caterer you admire. If you cannot find an internship, try volunteer work. Every community has food banks and prepared meals programs that could use some help. Hospitals and long-term care facilities also welcome volunteers. To make the experience count, be sure you are working directly with food in some way. Apply for part-time or summer work. Possibilities include working as an assistant caterer, a prep cook, or on the production line in a food company. Make sure you network and make contacts wherever you go. If you work hard and display enthusiasm, you may even be offered a full-time position.

College Career Center

Your college career center should be your first stop. You will find job boards with new openings posted as well as notices of recruiters that may be planning to visit the campus. Talk to your counselors about your career goals. They may have some ideas that you have not thought of.

Network

Networking is the key to any successful career and home economics is no exception. In fact, most professionals working in this field get more work through referrals than any other source. Jobs are often not posted publicly, but rather internally within companies and mentioned at social events. Finding a job is often a simple matter of knowing the right person at the right time. Start building your list of contacts in school. Include both your instructors and classmates. Instructors usually know many people in the industry, making them a valuable point of contact. You never know when a former classmate might be the next celebrity chef or magazine publisher. Expand your network by including anyone in the food industry – chefs, cooks, caterers, publicists, food distributors, and so on.

Job Boards

Looking for a job online can be tricky. If you search for "home economics" job, it is unlikely anything will turn up. But there are literally thousands of jobs available if you know how to find them. To get better results, search for the specific job title that interests you. For example, a search of "test kitchen assistant" is likely to yield 1,000 or more employers that are currently hiring.

Start Anywhere

Take advantage of any opportunities that come your way. Most professionals in this field get their start in low-level positions and work their way up the ladder. For example, recipe developers may start out as assistant caterers, research chefs begin as sous chefs, food technologists first work in institutional cafeterias, and magazine writers try their hand at blogging.

Narrow Your Focus

Some areas of the industry are hotter than others. Look for specific niche markets where your expertise can make you a desirable candidate. Food companies, restaurants, and medical facilities are constantly searching for new and exciting recipes for people following specific diets. Whether it is gluten-free, vegan, kosher, paleo, or low-carb, learning how to develop recipes that accommodate particular diet restrictions will impress companies that serve niche consumer preferences.

Stay Up to Date

You can stay abreast of the latest industry trends by visiting the websites of professional organizations. Read trade magazines regularly. That is where you will learn of new food publications that may be seeking recipes, packaged food companies that want to launch new products, or even fast food chains that want to experiment with new, exciting menu offerings.

You will notice there are help wanted ads in trade magazines, but they are usually aimed at seasoned professionals, not beginners.

ASSOCIATIONS

■ **American Association of Family & Consumer Sciences (AAFCS)**
http://www.aafcs.org

■ **Institute of Food Technologists**
www.ift.org

■ **American Institute of Wine and Food (AIWF)**
http://www.aiwf.org

■ **Research Chefs Association**
http://www.culinology.com

■ **Food Policy Action**
http://foodpolicyaction.org

PERIODICALS

■ **Food Manufacturing**
http://www.foodmanufacturing.com

■ **Still Life With**
http://stilllifewith.com

■ **Food Business Review**
http://www.food-business-review.com

■ **Food Processing**
http://www.foodprocessing.com

■ **The Cook's Cook**
http://thecookscook.com

WEBSITES

■ **Home Economics Careers & Technology**
http://www.hect.org

■ **America's Test Kitchen**
http://www.americastestkitchen.com

www.ingramcontent.com/pod-product-compliance
Lightning Source LLC
Chambersburg PA
CBHW061238180526
45170CB00003B/1350

* 9 7 8 1 5 4 6 8 3 7 3 8 1 *